WAR OF GRACE

POEMS FROM THE FRONT LINES OF RECOVERY

Dedicated to the many men who have graduated from Helping Up Mission - you give us courage for the fight.

Sic semper draconis

War of Grace
© Helping Up Mission 2016.
Website: helpingupmission.org

Helping Up
Mission™

Since 1885, Helping Up Mission has provided hope to people
experiencing homelessness, poverty or addiction by meeting their
physical, psychological, social and spiritual needs.

Cover art by Mark Ramiro
Cover design & typesetting by Vic King
Edited by Gary Johnson, Sean Parks, Greg Lattin,
Charles Arbogast, Yasin Abdul Adl, and Vic King
Printed in the PRC
ISBN: 978-0-9972604-0-3
Second edition. Thanks to Earl Hoopes for compiling the first.

CONTENTS

Foreword

Shadows

Guilt Quilt   11

Dark Skies   12

Drowning My Demons   13

A Symphony of Heroin   14

Wrongful Adrenaline Rush   15

Treatment   16

Black Heart   17

Dope Fiend Dreams   18

Reflections

We Wear a Mask   21

The Looking Glass To My Soul   22

Untitled   23

All The Pretty Ponies   24

Tired of Counterfeit   25

Mirrors   26

Surrender

Peace Be Still   29

From Heaven's Door   30

Letting It Go   31

In the Potter's Hand   32

Music Of Your Soul   33

The Prodigal Son   34
The Courtship   35
Silence   36
The Conqueror   39
Change   40

Musings

The Days of Yesteryear   45
The American Dream   46
And Now to Life   47
Untitled   48
Unknown Poet   50
Unknown Leader   51
HUM Limericks   52

Tainted Love

Jezebel   55
Freedom   56
The Break-Up   57
Love/Hate   59
Harmony   60
The Break-Up Letter   62

Conquest

The Price Paid   67
The Valley is the Peak   68
Pressure   69
The Everlasting Tree   70
An Autumn Mourning   71
Climbing Ever Upwards   72
To Die Like Autumn   75

Afterword

Poems by Author

FOREWORD

Many years ago, we began a poetry night at HUM because we saw poetry as a medium for opening souls, allowing their creativity and pain to spill, and wounds to slightly heal by this release. We believe this because this is what poetry has done for us and has done for many.

We hoped, and now have seen, how each man is more passionate and creative than he thought, and that each has something extraordinary to share. We hoped that they could see that poetry could be as simple as a haiku or as complex as a coupled rhyme; something as complex as love and life or as simple as "Ode to an Old Sock." We have all been startled by the powerful written voice of a timid, insecure man and the tender, sweet voice of a hardened addict. We have heard many a poetic thanks for the appearance of Christ in a man's life.

We have laughed together and we have cried together. Thank you for blessing us with your time and talent. Now thank you for sharing it here in written words with others.

Bob and Terri Smith
Poets and Volunteers

SHADOWS

Guilt Quilt

Gregory Lattin

It keeps in the cold and shuts everyone out
Alone with my anguish, self loathing, and doubt
Scraps of sorrow, remnants of shame
Shredded ambitions, knots tied with pain
Folded up neatly and placed on the shelf
I pull it down daily to hide from myself

Dark Skies
Charles Arbogast

As clouds roll in and skies turn black
When a beautiful day becomes as dark as night
No ray of sun to guide my plight
As I try to walk through the dark
With a matchbook light
The darkness creeps to snuff out my sight

This nocturnal world has become my home
This place of shadows a comfort zone
As monsters come I transform into my own
And to survive this eternal dark
Fangs and claws have grown

I adapted to this place that I lived for years
Where the rain that fell
Was from this lost soul's tears
And then one day, a forgotten light appears
The clouds burn away and blue skies become clear

Drowning My Demons
Kenneth Partyka

Demons with scuba tanks
Swimming around
I feel like I'm the one
That's being drowned
So I seek out higher ground
And change my plan of attack
And I'll be damned
If they didn't grow huge wings of black

I felt so hollow, like an empty shell
Was I bound to follow my own road to hell
I felt so hopeless and in despair
As I sat with an empty stare
Drowning my demons was a pack of lies
With my stinking breath and bloodshot eyes
My demons were only getting bigger
And I was only killing my liver

A Symphony of Heroin

Charles Arbogast

Days go by and still I think of you
Days go by when I couldn't live my life without you
The false joy and true pain that lingers on my mind
I gave you my heart and hopes and dreams

You gave me a false sense of worth
And none of it was real
I think of me trapped in the dark
You were my light, my light
When I was alone and you weren't with me
The darkness consumed me

They say the night is darkest just before the dawn
You kept me in this pre-mourning state for years on end
Waiting for a sunrise that never came
And only once the drugs are gone
I'd feel like dying, I'd feel like dying

You stole everything from me like a thief in the night
My pride, my integrity, my soul
Is it worth it, can you even hear me
Standing with your spotlight on me

It's 4 o'clock in the f***in' morning
Each day gets more like the last day
And now I can see it coming
When I'm standing in this river drowning

This could be my chance to say good-bye
And now I'm ready to be free
I'm ready to break free of these chains of bondage that
you've had me in

So I'm as free as a bird now
And this bird you cannot change.

Wrongful Adrenaline Rush
Steve Shirk

Jumping out of a plane
Falling fast, stress running
Through my views, injecting speed.
Derailing, crashing, pulling me in
Falling faster and faster, death comes in
The Grim Reaper ready to take me as I sin.

Thoughts are willing, action is killing
One last breath tonight, I'm willing
Life slipping, catching a high, catching a ride
Blood stops pumping, gonna die
Feel a jolt, see the light
God looking down, saying it's not your night.
It's not your night.

Treatment
Gregory Lattin

My life was once filled with color and lights
Dark, dreary days and calliope-tuned nights
Up, up the mountain I'd race from below
To summit the vista and drown in its snow

I would dance and would frolic in the dizzying height
The air thin and cold like a murderer's knife
And from that sharp edge, I heard a voice from below
First beckoning sweetly, then a furious bellow

"You've danced and you've played
Now it's time to come home
Remember how much you loved being alone?"
I recalled the soft warmth of the valley so dark
The sadness, the sorrow like a day in the park

So down I flew into my favorite hollow
My sty full of filth and depression to wallow
A noose round my neck like a diamond of hope
I might as well hang since I have so much rope

But then you appeared all jaundiced and mellow
I thought "How'd you guess my favorite color is yellow?"
At first fifty MGs and soon fifty more
You clipped off my wings so I no longer soar

A once-gilded bird now I'm gelded as f***
I'm on a plateau, I am stagnant and stuck
My life once had color but now it's all grays
As I float through life in my Zoloft haze

So no more warm valleys or dizzying heights
The doctors came in and shut off the lights
I sit here all smiles with a halcyon glow
But I miss the mountains and the valleys below

Black Heart
Jerry Fullbright

My black heart is all I see
It's dark as a lonesome hall
So black inside, where could I be
I reach out for you and fall

When the sun goes down
And the moon is bright
There are stars all around
But in my heart it's night

I look for you to give a tender shove
But my heart's so dark that it can't touch love
There is no vision of a pony ride
It's a dark collision, heart's black inside

I can't recall a lighted night
Where the moon stands tall
And the stars shine bright
This black heart has a power unknown
I did this myself, no love and alone

Dope Fiend Dreams
Timothy B. Farrare

Dope fiend dreams, late nights and long days
Blinded by darkness, praying for better ways.
Fading in and out, caught in the fog,
Dope man hits my phone and I leap like a frog.

Caught in this storm, I can feel the waves rumble
Pills, weed, and drink are the predators in my jungle.
Deserving more, but settling for less…
These sleepless nights, dying for rest.

In need of a miracle
God please hear my prayers;
Running rivers flow
With no love to sooth these tears.

Dope fiend dreams, haunted by my past,
Inside, my body's yelling "Is this time the last?"
Can't see my future, it's looking very bleak,
But if I walk by faith and not sight,
Our Father I'll surely meet.

REFLECTIONS

We Wear a Mask
Anonymous

We wear the mask that grins and lies
It hides our cheeks and shades our eyes
This debt we pay to human guile
With torn and bleeding hearts we smile
And mouth with myriad subtleties

Why should the world be over-wise
In counting all our tears and sighs
Nay, let them only see us, while
We wear the mask that grins and lies

We smile, but O great Christ, our cries
To Thee from tortured souls arise
We sing, but oh the clay is vile
Beneath our feet, and long the mile
But let the world dream otherwise,
We wear the mask that grins and lies.

The Looking Glass To My Soul
Charles Arbogast

As I looked in the mirror
I couldn't believe the things I saw.
The pain inside my blue eyes
The cracks and empty space inside my wall.
The sounds of tears and mother's sighs.
All my regrets and all my pain
Have me trapped, stuck in the rain.
The emptiness inside my soul
I'm lost in space, my own black hole.
I've given up on myself
My hopes and dreams set on a shelf
I feel so lost, nowhere to turn.
Get one more at any cost, what bridge I'll burn.
But now as I stand in front of the looking glass,
That me is gone. That was my past.

Untitled
Charles Chapman

Alone again in the dark
I examine my rage
It feels like two people
Locked in a cage
As both try to break free
They destroy one another
Until all that remains
Is this little thing, smothered

Overwhelmed by the past
I look to let go
To change who I am
To change what I know
I was born in a kingdom
Desolate
And bare
I'll ascend to a kingdom
Lavished with care

There's a place for this animal
The one that remains
I've become a new creature
Born of Christ
With no shame

All The Pretty Ponies

Charles Arbogast

I guess you could have called me an urban cowboy
How quickly I fell in love
The first time climbing up on that white pony
The way it filled the void inside my soul
The way it felt like a thousand railroad trains
Turning away with my fear, pain, regrets
And filled me with the thing I thought I lacked
Confidence, joy, love.

But then the joy of riding those ponies went away
As that feeling of freedom
became a monkey on my back
And as I climbed aboard that train
Leaving the station
I was told, "This is where you get off."

As I looked around at this post-war city
I thought *How can this be?*
All this pain and destruction was done by me.
So now, as the white pony still runs wild and free
I've finally decided the cowboy life is not for me.

Tired of Counterfeit
Damien Smith

I'm sick of trying to pretend
While blowing in the wind
Wit so called friends
Storytellers wit ah fake grin
Remember lying is a sin
And God your best friend

Truth against lies
And you know who win
You betta ask God
And repent for your sin
Before it's too late
And the devil trap you in

Speaking the truth
Through his word is the proof
We should listen up
Before the Christians go poof
They're gone, nowhere to be found
Then we're left behind
Not knowing what to do

So I gotta get myself straight
Before it's too late
And then I'm stuck on the other side
Looking through Heaven's gate
And Hell be my fate
Wit no faith
Millions can relate
Dying of thirst
Leaves my spirit to ache

Mirrors

Timothy B. Farrare

Mirror, Mirror on the wall,
      inside can you see?
The anger, depression, and pain that burns
      deep where others fail to see.
Mirror, mirror on the wall,
      who am I to you?
A loser, user, and abuser
      stuck together like glue.

Mirror, mirror on the wall,
      can you see the madness and rage?
Outside I seem fine,
      but inside covered with flames!
Mirror, mirror on the wall,
      how do I fix this ugly mess?
By realizing I'm God's student,
      and this is another test.

SURRENDER

Peace Be Still
Dale C. Keels

A gust of the wind swept over the land
The earth buckled in, and the trees couldn't stand
Within a small town, it brought a quickening breeze
It never slowed down, and the ground began to freeze

It had the power to move you, like nobody knows
It could've blown straight through you
If that's what it chose

But I've read a story about a powerful man
That was raised to glory, with all power in His hand
He is that same Man, and it's the same breeze
This is the same land that will bow to its knees

He has that same power, He has that same will
He is that strong tower that said "Peace be still."

From Heaven's Door
Edward Ostrowski

How can you see a sunrise through a storm?
Or look beyond a scornful face
And find a heart that's torn?
When strangers sense that you have something more
Don't walk by sight, just gaze from Heaven's door

If evil men surround you, front and back
And it seems you're not prepared for their attack
Don't be defeated, looking lowly towards the floor
You're not alone, just gaze from Heaven's door

The simple of the world confound the wise
True beauty is not seen through shallow eyes
And a rich man think he's better than the poor
But his soul is empty
If you just gaze from Heaven's door

Not all is what it seems through faithless eyes
When you walk by sight, you buy the devil's lies
But faith is what the Lord is waiting for
Then all things are possible
If you just gaze from Heaven's door

Letting It Go
Dale C. Keels

We worry about tomorrow
But our tomorrow should hold no fear
We've been bottled up with sorrow
But tomorrow will soon be here

Shackled with devastation
In hopes that tomorrow will pass
Startled by old temptations
That remind us of our past

Temptations are just a trial
Simple patterns we've come to know
Number one is our own denial
Let's recover by letting it go

In the Potter's Hand

Edward Ostrowski

Molded in the Potter's hand
A fallen soul can surely stand
He found me broken, worn, and rough
A heart so empty and void of love
Covered with dust, clear to the bone
Surrounded by others, but still so alone

Searching through life for a peaceful place
Condemned by the low, knowing nothing of grace
A mind so distraught, of such a low self esteem
Not a friend by my side, or so it had seemed
Destined for hell, but what did I know?
I reached the end of my rope, and chose to let go

Then He reached down His arm, into that miry pit
He said, I'm your only chance, won't you take it?
He pulled me on up and shook the dust from my soul
In the hand of the Potter, He began shaping His goal
As he patiently worked, from the inside on out
I could see in His eyes, He hadn't a doubt

The process was painful, it took pressure and time
But just like the diamond, I was beginning to shine
Little by little, I am changed everyday
I'm not what I was, but I'm still only clay
One thing I have learned, that few understand
The molding never stops, when I'm in the Potter's hand.

Music Of Your Soul

Dawn Sherwood

You'd be surprised what God has shown me
Through the music of your soul
To see the beauty that lies deep in you
And all the love that you will know
It may be covered up with injuries
You may not see it for yourself
But I not only saw, I felt it
I've known some of your pain myself

I wanna thank you now
And make you hear you're someone
Loving, kind and dear
You'd be surprised the secrets God reveals
Through the music of your soul

Your aches and pains
Your fears and secret loves
Are closer than you seem to know
You thought you'd buried them, but he knows them all
They are music of your soul

Ah the music
I hear the music
Mmm the music of your soul

The Prodigal Son
Edward Ostrowski

There I did lay, a sinful disgrace
I certainly did not reflect your face
I wallowed in shame of unheavenly thoughts
I've reaped and I've sown the evil I wrought
I've plundered my spoils, I've squandered my wealth
I've quenched the Spirit and destroyed my own health
I moan and I groan in the mire and muck
I cleave to the dust and I can't get unstuck

Who can release me of this pathetic condition?
I've fallen so low, I'm barely existing
I'm deceitfully wicked, I'm cruel as the grave
I not only served sin, I became its damn slave
I'm chained and I'm bound of my own free will
I was seconds from suicide, all time had stood still
Then you brought your arm low to the pit I was in
You ripped me away from the bondage of sin

You bathed me in love and caressed me with grace
And moment by moment I resembled your face
You melted my heart and made it brand new
The old man had died, now my soul longed for you
Words can't explain the freedom you give
You abolished my sin and now I can live
This prodigal son you have brought home at last
In the arms of my Father, no joy can surpass

It's true, yes it's true, there's no hope without you
If not for your love, what on earth would I do?

The Courtship
Gary Johnson

How do I start to love you?
Where does our conversation begin?
I heard about your past relationships
Through songs and books
And millions in buildings swearing - you are good
How good you were to them
How you held them
In their time of need
And that you were a great listener

I heard you sacrificed someone dear to you
To spend time with me
That means you don't mind sharing
My horoscope sign is Gemini
Heard yours was Alpha and Omega
Well we should get alone
For a long time
My hobbies are worshipping and praise
I heard you've done some services
In your time

We have so much in common
I feel like we were created
In image and likeness
We do have a lot in common
I don't know about my feelings
But it sure sounds like you love me

Silence
Charles Chapman

All I feel is rage
All these walls
All I see is a cage

Is it just me?
My mind playing tricks?
Is it the devil interceding my destiny?

(silence)

Where are you God?
You said you'd be here!
My smile's a façade
Maybe I'm too dark for you to hear?

(silence)

All of my sins
You've turned away
You did the same to your own son
He rose, but me, I'm still a slave?

(silence)

Slave to self
Slave to the chaos
I thought you were here

(silence)

I've been alone all my life
This feels different
These emotions, this strife
Hello! Are you there?

(silence)

As much as I want to
I will not quit
I have to believe you brought me here
Am I still part of your plan?

(silence)

Is it tears you need from me?
I've surrendered everything!
I've nothing else to offer you.
Still listening, Lord?

(silence)

Please take this pain
Excuse me, I mean rage
My bad, I meant fear
What am I feeling?

(silence)

What do I do?
I can't do this alone
No one understands me
No one knows my pain

(silence)

Guess it's just me alone, wandering, a ghost, invisible, no destiny...

(shoosh!)

Lord?

I am here my son
Never have I left you
I've built your path
You have to walk it
Experience these things yourself
You're fighting for your soul
I won't give up on you
Stand fast and stay strong
This too shall pass
You're going to make it
Just hold on and believe
Hold on to your faith
Behold the glory of the Lord
For you, my son, are a miracle
I love you, my son.

(speechless)

The Conqueror
Charles Arbogast

As I step out in the light to see
Who's this in the mirror looking back at me?
I ponder who can this impostor be?
Behind him a world of catastrophe
I wonder what could have caused this atrocity
It was his pride and bellicosity
His indifference for others and animosity

And as his frozen heart begins to thaw
Up from the depths, on hands and knees he crawls
And even when he slips and falls
He stays his course until he comes upon a titanic wall
"I need your help, God"
He says in a pleading call
Just as, brick by brick, it begins to fall
If you put your faith in him you can conquer all.

Change
David Ford

As I look in the mirror
I don't like what I see
Or what has become
Of this man in front of me
Deep in his eyes
I see sorrow and pain
Asking himself, *Will this ever change?*

I have cried out for help
So many times
But there's no one to hear me
It's like I am a mime
I tell myself I am a loser
That I am too far gone
Out here on the streets
No longer have a home

I now find my pleasures
In needle, spoon, and pill
That's the only way I know
To hide how I feel
My life is now darker
Than it's ever been
I'm ready to quit
On a fight I can't win

Then from the darkness
A voice calls my name
Telling me he'll take
My sorrow and pain

I lowered my head
With tears on my face
Too afraid to lift it
For shame and disgrace

"I'm not worthy Lord
You should pass me on by"
He said "I won't do that
It's for you, son, I died"
Then he took my hand
And released all my tension
He led me up here
To Helping Up Mission

And though I have only
A short time clean
I can do all things
Through Christ who strengthens me
So if you are someone
Held by these same chains
Turn them over to Him
And your life he will change

MUSINGS

The Days of Yesteryear
Harold Duppins

Whatever happened to the days of yesteryear
When life was simple without any fear?
Watching little tikes
Riding little bikes
Children of all ages enjoying the sun
Running and laughing, having innocent fun

Whatever happened to the days of yesteryear
When love was honest, enduring and sincere?
It was cool to carry your girlfriend's books
Didn't matter if the guys laughed
And gave you silly looks

Black and white TV
Was fine with me

Didn't know about AIDS, was that a foreign policy?
But I did know that war was a certain reality
Sandlot baseball was my favorite thing
Only had one bat that someone would bring

A Friday night party I didn't want to miss
Hoping I'd get my very first kiss
Listening to music of love and romance
Waiting for the right girl to ask for a dance

Whatever happened to the days of yesteryear
When life was simple without any fear
Sad to say, but they are no longer here

The American Dream
Brian Vincer

The gears turn, friction degrading
The product is lost, slowly fading
They fall to the floor, damage done
Coexistence

When beauty and love become a myth
As does our foundation, the gears grip
Self-preservation overshadows passion
Revolution is a must

Our neglected toys on the top shelf
Riddled with dust of industrialization
Come now, to my realization
If this machine is to run
Our consciousness must become one!
Turn away from yesterday!
Tomorrow is in our hands!

And Now to Life
David Abrahams

Some say life is all too short
I have only two questions
"Why do you believe the word 'short' has direction?"
"Or is it because of the pain in 'life'
that you disrespect its aggression?"
It matters not of your preference,
Or if you answer the questions

The truth is objective
Don't try to object it
Your words are subjective
My method is message
Truth valid respected
A fool would reject this
A wise man would test it

If you're washed in His blood
Time is a gift
Not an incentive.

Untitled

Jason Norwood

Standing on this rooftop
In this beautifully broken home
My city all around me
As far as my eye could roam

The lights and the chatter
Streaming through my mind
The things I can remember
And some I've left behind

There's a quiet desperation
Hanging in the air
Things seem to be in ruins
And it smells of disrepair

There's roads down there, so many roads
That I've often traveled on
A bad turn here, a bad turn there
And I wonder where I've gone

The city lights so bright
They seemed to sing out my name
The side streets so bleak and dark
And always filled with shame

But there's good in this city!
There's a desire which still burns
And it's hidden in plain sight
Around every twist and turn

So don't just stand there angry
And think what this city's done to you
This city has its own life
And you hurt it a little too

So I'll be standing on this rooftop
In this perfect time and place
I'll pray for my city
And gladly defend its case

Unknown Poet
Gary Johnson

My proudest moment is now
Listen as the bell tolls for the final hour
I live a sinner
I die a poet
My voice cracked and vibrating
Through the halls of learning
I need no governor's stay
I go shamelessly
This is my fate
Your last sight of me

There will be no buildings erected
No bust created
No tears shed
No literary legacy left behind
Deemed a heretic
Blasphemous, they claim
Erased from the Book of Life

I wrote to enlighten them
Not against them
Saying what their hearts felt
But mouths couldn't say
The poison I take eases their conscience
So let laughter and celebration fill your hearts
Tell all what you have witnessed here
Ah, freed soul
I am innocent, but guilty of thinking for myself

Unknown Leader
Everett Smith

I'd rather see a sermon than hear one any day;
I'd rather one should walk with me
Than merely show me the way.
The eye's a better pupil and more willing than the ear;
Fine counsel is confusing but example is always clear.

And the best of all the preachers
Are the men who live their creed.
Son, to see good put into action
Is what everybody needs.
I soon can learn to do it if you'll let me see it done;
I can see your hands in action,
But your tongue too fast may run.

And the lectures you deliver may be very fine and true;
But I'd rather get my lesson by observing what you do.
For I may not understand you
And the high advice you give;
But there's no misunderstanding how you act and live.

HUM Limericks
Gregory Lattin

There once was a pastor named Gary
Whose head was both shiny and hairy.
He's addicted to Jesus
And the lessons he'll teach us
Will lessen the burdens we carry.

There once was a preacher called Rallo.
God's word every day he does follow.
He yells "Do you hear me?"
If not, well, you should be.
Or forever in shame you will wallow.

There once was a chaplain named Vic
Whose beard was so long and so thick.
He plays the ukulele,
And ministers daily.
To bring help to the homeless and sick.

There once was a man called Charles Duffy
Whose beard grew in scraggly and scruffy.
He lives at the HUM,
And gives towels to a bum.
I guess you could say he was lucky.

There once was a guy called Renard
Who hit the crack pipe pretty hard.
He said "Jesus make me
The man that I should be."
Now heaven's his eternal reward.

TAINTED LOVE

Jezebel
Dale C. Keels

How many men has she taken the time
To mess up their life and torment their mind
"It just happens to be," as she'd like to say
"It wasn't just me, it just happened that way"

"I brought to his life the stars and the sky"
"He left his wife, for it was not I"
"It wasn't intended to go that way"
"As our love grew, he just happened to stay"
"I really don't love him, and that is a fact"
"If she thinks that much of him, she'll take him back"

I'd like to explain how these things occur
They're all quite the same, and they all will leave her
"Do I really care? I'd rather not tell"
"Anytime that I can," signed: Jezebel

Freedom
Charles Arbogast

As I let my lungs fill up with smoke
And you've got my veins all tangled closed
I start shaking at the thought
'Cause you are everything I'm not

You were there to bring me joy in the sadness
A candle in the window on the cold dark nights
But you didn't think I could tell
That you were trying to make a fool out of me

I started to believe your lies and false promises
The candle you once were, was lost
in the tornado you became
as you ripped apart the town
in the wake of your destruction

But I rebuilt all that I've lost
I still miss you like a flower
Misses the sunshine on an overcast day
But if you love something, let it free

So now this freedom I'm asking
It didn't come cheap
My heart, my soul, has been paid
I break loose of your hold
That's an even trade
I need to depart from the life we've made

The Break-Up
Harold Duppins

There was a time that we were inseparable
My love for you was such that I couldn't live without you
I cherished you with all my time, all my willingness
I was so obsessed with you
That I was blinded by my own lust
Tortured by an uncontrollable need
To always have you near

I clung to you like a child with a new toy
Never wanting to let you go
Never wanting you out of my life
My heart and my mind was a batch of emotions
Thrown together in a mass of confusion

My eyes slowly became open
And I could see the reality of you
I could see the false love, the false passion
That captured me like a young lion
That strayed away from his mother

The more I saw less of you, the less I needed you
You can no longer seduce me
Nor tempt me with your deadly passions
I will no longer search for you
Nor call out to you in the middle of the night

I will not be persuaded by memories of past love for you
Our relationship has come to its end
I have a new love who is faithful and loving to me
She will not invade my heart with false hopes
Her name is Sobriety

The Great Deception
Charles Arbogast

You whisper wicked words
That weave and wind their way into my mind
Like waves washing over white sand weathering a storm
Your beautiful benevolence
Breaking the barriers of my logic
As I listen intently with intrigue in insolation
They engulf my intellect with indecision

You lie through your teeth
You're not at all what you seem
And everybody knows you're a liar
So why don't I?

Your talented tongue twists
And tangles my thoughts
As you tempt me with tantalizing talk
As a serpent slithers and squirms
Through short shrubs
Seeking an unsuspecting squirrel
To circle and spew venom into its life source

Now you're lying through teeth
You're not at all what you seem
And everybody knows you're a liar
Why don't I?

You manipulate my mind with malicious motives.
The chaos you create
Is like a cataclysmic collision of cars
Crashing head on.

I know you're lying through your teeth
You weren't at all what you seemed
And everybody knows you're a liar
And so do I.

Love/Hate
Charles Arbogast

You love me, you hate me
You degrade me, betray me, forsake me
I thought I was love struck
But now I'm just f***ed up.
Got me looking at the world as an empty cup.

At first we were perfect
Then you made me feel I'm worthless
Lost with no purpose
You used to keep me warm at night
Morning comes, once again another fight
Now we are losing sight of a future that looked bright
Standing at this crossroad
Which way to turn - left or right?

And all your love I tried to earn
Now becomes hate, I've learned
I've made a choice, grabbing gas and matches
This is a bridge I'll burn
I know our paths were entwined in fate
Now that you're gone, my life is great
And you're still the one I love and hate.

Harmony
Anonymous

Breathing, so slightly, so softly
watching you smile in your dream
A gentle curl falls silently across your brow
caressing your cheek, flowing lazily around your face
to the corner of your mouth, kissing your pouty lips…

Breathing, so slightly, so softly
As a willow's in the distance, weeping, though panes
of paint speckled glass, shimmers with the
rustlin' wind, reaching down to a bed of grass
spreading out into the ripples of the creek…and

Breathing, so slightly, so softly,
As a sauntering goose lazily glides by, its young
gosling covered in her quilted wing, shielded
from the random gusts, fussing unconcernedly
at little ones stride, squawking, beckoning
inadvertently loving, guiding her love
hastily to the shelter of the willow…and

Breathing, so slightly, so softly
A stirring form deep within, you jostle, shiver
groan, your milky smooth skin becomes like
gooseflesh, down your lovely neck and arms.
I cover you quietly, lightly, tenderly, the warmth
of the heavy quilt comforts you, you draw
it up tightly over your freckled shoulder,

I whisper, barely, into your ear "it's only the
wind my love". You find your peaceful
dream again, Am I there with you?

A turned up smile and the faint flitter of
Your eyelids tells me, Yes! And I am here with you.
still Breathing, so slightly, so softly – Loving You,
Wanting you, Needing you, more than words can say

My eyes peer again to the clattering window, I find
beside the willow, a lone flower, bent low, fighting
bravely against the ever increasing wind, none but
a few petals remain, fiercely hanging on, but even still,

Breathing, so slightly, so softly
I walk to the sill and admire its strength
no one to cover, or shield, or love its
Chills bring my arms up to embrace myself
I mutter despairingly through the glass
Sometimes it seems we must face the storms alone
I feel the warmth of your quilt laid upon my back

I turn to you slowly as you gather me into your arms
Together we gaze out, wrapped in warmth
A sudden ray of sunlight burst from the sky, upon
the lone flower, its weary frail stem straightens
in relief as it sways in the sun, it turns
upward toward the heavens in its loving reply
for that brief moment it seems, all of creation did
groan collectively, In a perfect harmony of love

You whisper delicately into my ear
As long as you are loved you will never be alone
Clinging together, ever still…
Breathing, so slightly…
        so softly…

The Break-Up Letter
Edward Ostrowski

Goodbye, so long, the end
I'm sorry but I never want to see you again
Why'd you have to hurt me so bad?
Why'd you have to take everything I ever had?
The way things turned out, I never did expect
I gotta' get out of this mess with a shred of self-respect
So goodbye, so long, the end

You were my companion, my lover, and my friend
I kept you close to me, I thought I'd have you till the end
I let you make all the decisions, I played by all the rules
And now I finally realize you played me like a fool

It aches for me to walk away, it sickens me to death
But if I don't break this chain of bondage
You'll take my very last breath
So goodbye, so long, the end
I'm sorry, but I never want to see you again

I wish I could say I'll miss you
And part of me will never forget
There were times when only you comforted me
But even that I will always regret

I'm moving on to brighter days
My eyes are clean without the haze
I'm dreaming to be the man
Who's free of these conditions
So I'll talk to you straight and to the point
I don't need this drug addiction

So goodbye, so long, the end
My eyes are so much cleaner
And you never were my friend
So goodbye, so long, the end

CONQUEST

The Price Paid

Charles Chapman

As I seek my purpose
As I look to its intent
As I look over my past
And all the torment
You would think that I'd learn
All the mistakes that I've made
With this life's twists and turns
It's not just me who has paid.

My kids pay the price
My kids feel the pain
They need their protector
Of which I've abstained
Each day that I'm gone
I'm growing in God
I know they're not alone
My God it's so hard.

I pray I repent
I give you this soul
So take my resentments
My past I let go
Transform this guy
To the man I must be
Transform my soul
To the man my kids need.

The Valley is the Peak
Edward Ostrowski

You have conquered that mountain
Or so you have thought
But it was through the ravine
Where your victory was wrought
For the place you've been brought to
Is not the place where you have won
T'was at the foot of the hill
Where your trial begun
For God sees us strong
When we seem the most weak
'Cause in the eyes of the Lord
The valley is the peak.

In our lives there are mountains
Unsurpassable walls
We may soar high above them
With no resistance or falls
But our victories are not measured
By mere daily success
For it's the triumphant believer
Who has endured great duress
Hardships and trials, struggles and griefs
Life's daily pressures, beyond our belief
From broken and humble
To compassionate and meek
You may rest upon the mountain
But the valley is the peak.

I know such a Man
Well acquainted with grief
He suffered all his life

For those in unbelief
All the sins of the world
Were placed upon this Man
In the valley of sin and death
He revealed His Father's plan
And on that cross, in horrid pain
He displayed by what He would speak
You're delivered to the mountain
But the valley is the peak.

Pressure
Jerry Fullbright

Every day there is pressure on me
Even when it's not important therein
It gets so bad, and only I can see
How the walls are caving in

Sometimes it's just sad, and only I can say
How it gets so bad that I can't pray it away
And there are times when I feel
Life is over and done
The pressure is real, but I overcome

But why feel pressure in such a beautiful land
And it comes whenever, and I don't understand
But there's always tomorrow
And I will face that pressure
I'll hold on with no sorrow,
And won't let go never

The Everlasting Tree
Robert Montgomery

Though the wind blows
And the rain still comes and goes
The tree still stands and the tree still grows
Though the seasons change and the old leaves fade away
The tree still stands and the tree still remains
When darkness is all around, no sunlight shines down
The tree still stands tall throughout the town
When death seems to consume
Every single thing that moved
The tree still stood and the tree still grew

The ability to survive was already in the roots
Plus God's hand was upon that tree and that's the truth
No matter what environment the tree was residing in
It still grew higher than the average expected
There's no stopping it
Sky is the limit, that means infinite elevation
Rise again when they thought it was over
Surprise them haters, this tree was designed to make it

Against all odds
Stay alive, motivated inside
Repopulate the population
The last of a dying breed
Cause ain't too many nowadays
Built like that special tree
Damaged but not destroyed
Hurt but not killed
The seed's already been planted and the root's too real

The foundation is too strong
To ever let this tree stop growing
And even to this day the tree still lives on
'Cause I am the tree in the human form
Still rising over the earth, moon, and stars
Or whatever's in my way
I go above and beyond

An Autumn Mourning
Charles Arbogast

As the days grow short and get brisk
And all the leaves begin to change hues
Will the reward outweigh the risk?
Times grow hard: what road to choose?

Will I open up Pandora's Box
To open up this cellar door?
Will I invite in this cunning fox,
Let in this boy that rots my core?

Do I remain on this hard and rocky path
Or take the route where I know the way?
Just give in and feel the wrath?
I'll ask God to help me through this autumn day

I will not fold like a house of cards
To be steadfast when times get hard

Climbing Ever Upwards
Dan Sharrar

You
You have been here since the beginning
You were once low, an urchin, a serf
But not for long
You have risen

You have brought yourself up from the dirt and the filth
You have scrabbled, clawed, and fought for every breath
Every scrap
Every glimpse of sunlight

And as you dragged yourself up from the pits
You have seen the faces of the masses
Your enemies
Your friends
Your family
Your teachers
Your demons
You have taken them in
Taken their measure
Gazed long into their eyes and seen their souls

When you broke free of the nostril-clogging dirt,
You did not stop
With nothing but wide-open plains before you,
You staggered
Fell to your knees
Wept at the sight of the wide open sky
You raised your hands to the sun and you cried out

You gave voice to your struggle
Sang your song to the heavens
When you had no breath left in you,
You rose to your feet
You took one look around you
Chose a direction, and RAN
Your feet pounding the plains
The wind washing the dirt from your hair
Tears of joy cleansing your face, you ran
You ran until the surface of the plains broke
And gave way to forest
You leapt over roots
Swung from the branches
And laughed as the deer and foxes kept pace

That night you slept in the tallest branches
The full moon wrapping you in a blanket of light
Cool spring water refreshed you in the morning
and freedom filled your veins

The muck and the mire of your past
Seemed a long-past nightmare
Dreamt by some other person
And as the forest gave way to foothills
And you gazed upon the mountaintops
You wished upon
Like stars as a child
You realized you were a fool to merely dream
To merely wish

The stars of today are the sunrises of the future
The sky darkens as you begin to climb,
And it worries you not
The clouds grow heavy with rain,

And it worries you not
The sky unleashes torrents, and it bothers you not
What is the weight of drops of water when you have felt
The weight of the earth itself?
What is the weight of a storm when you have felt
The weight of the grave?
Nothing
You climb
You fight
You struggle
You remember the faces of those long-past ghosts
And you smile

For once again, you find yourself
Hauling yourself ever upwards
Your hands filthy, your chest heaving
The memory of breaking free of the earth
Is still fresh in your mind
Yours cheeks are still stained with tears of joy
First shed in the light of the sun
The song you sang to the heavens still rings in your ears
And as you climb
Avalanches tumbling down in your wake
Clouds parting like a crowd in awe of your passing
Your smile widens at the thought of what it will feel like
To sing your song from the top of this mountain

You
You are mighty
And you have been here since the beginning.

To Die Like Autumn
Bob Smith

I hope to die like Autumn
With such stubbornness and grace
Strut forth the colors in my hair
With lines etched in my face

Then stand with head held proudly
With arms lay thin with age
As the dancers have departed
Leaving props upon the stage

I hope to die like Autumn
Like a football field's last game
My heart stretched out a hundred yards
Cleats churning through the rain

And knowing all the damage
That my green turns into brown
But smiling as their passion
And their cheer seeps in my ground

I hope to die like Autumn
And its leaf still slightly gold
With skin a little thinner now
His grasp just taking hold

Then a strong wind breaks his tether
Now his death, a silent kill
And his course, the breeze's laughter
Till she lays him down so still

AFTERWORD

So many of the psalms are cries of David's heart to God. Words filled with a range of emotion – cries of faith, lament… and hope.

The words in this book are the cries of the men we have the privilege to walk alongside in that journey, not unlike David's walk in the wilderness. We believe that just as David got in touch with God in the wilderness, when men pour out their hearts on paper, it helps them connect with their true selves, their peers, and with their Creator God.

We have watched healing take place as words are written down – sometimes beautifully raw, but always with a sense of hope. We hope you enjoy these poems, and we look forward to sharing more with you.

Mike Rallo
Director of Spiritual Life

AUTHOR INDEX

Abrahams, David 47

Anonymous 21, 60

Arbogast, Charles 12, 14, 22, 24, 39, 56, 58, 59, 71

Chapman, Charles 23, 36, 67

Duppins, Harold 45, 57

Farrare, Timothy B. 18, 26

Ford, David 40

Fullbright, Jerry 17, 69

Johnson, Gary 35, 50

Keels, Dale C. 29, 31, 55

Lattin, Gregory 11, 16, 52

Montgomery, Robert 70

Norwood, Jason 48

Ostrowski, Edward 30, 32, 34, 62, 68

Partyka, Kenneth 13

Sharrar, Dan 72

Sherwood, Dawn 33

Shirk, Steve 15

Smith, Bob 75

Smith, Damien 25

Smith, Everett 51

Vincer, Brian 46

LEARN MORE

To learn more about Helping Up Mission, visit our website and join our community on social media:

Website	helpingupmission.org
Facebook	helpingupmission
Instagram	@helpingup
Twitter	@helpingup
Soundcloud	helpingup
Youtube	helpingupmission

If you are interested in volunteering or supporting our work financially, give us a call at 410-675-4357.

You can download the audiobook of this book at: helpingupmission.org/poems